THE

I0131845

BUSINESS

OF

PEOPLE

*PROVEN METHODS FOR INCREASING
LEADERSHIP AND EMPLOYEE
PERFORMANCE*

RAY HODGE

THE

BUSINESS

OF

PEOPLE

Edited by Janette Parr

Layout and Design by Thea Tagulao

ISBN 978-0-9943138-2-9

TABLE OF CONTENTS

TABLE OF CONTENTS

ABOUT THE AUTHOR

Ray Hodge's 'talent' is in working with individuals and organisations to help them both identify and realise their ideal future. He has the unique capacity to span the spheres of personal and organisational psychology along with tangible business process improvement – bringing together a powerful mix in his consultative, writing, coaching and advisory work.

He has the 'knack' of making the complex simple, identifying the primary obstacles blocking 'flow' that prevent both businesses and individuals from moving forward while creating significant and often dramatic results in the process.

He has worked with individuals, sole practitioners right the way through to the Department of the Prime Minister and Cabinet and much in between. He is a regular guest speaker with his writing appearing frequently in national publications. He has been interviewed internationally, cited on Forbes.com and is the author of Smash The Bottleneck that is available on Amazon.

He lives in Melbourne Australia, has four children and when he's not working he is likely to be exploring wineries, watching live music or dancing.

INTRODUCTION

Of the many things in life that fascinate me, people would have to be at the top of the list.

"Why did she do it that way?"

"What inspired him to think that?"

"Why did they choose that role and not the other?"

"Why are they so productive?"

"Why are they so happy when their lives appear to be in tatters?"

"Why are they always late?"

"That waiter made no impression on me yet the other made me want to return. What was the difference?"

In more than thirty years working with people, I have pondered these and countless other questions. And now, working with business owners, I hear statements like:

"I feel like all I do is run a crèche. I feel like I'm a babysitter, not a business owner."

"Business would be great if I didn't have to work with people."

INTRODUCTION

"I can never get anyone decent to work here."

"I could sack the lot of them."

And the most memorable: *"Everyone who works here is a d...head."*

There is, I have found, no business quite like the people business. For some business owners, their people are their greatest asset; for others, just a big thorn in their side, (paraphrased for nicety's sake). In my consulting work, process improvement is a relatively simple formula – if I change this input, it will deliver that output. But where people are involved, we often find ourselves venturing into the unknown.

What is contained here is gleaned from my work with many people over many years – getting the best out of others, helping people find their way in their lives, their careers, and their relationships, motivating the unmotivated, and engaging with a vast array of individuals. It is a collection of articles, most of which have been published in various forms. They are not designed to be read in sequence so if you're challenged with a particular area or a chapter title grabs your fancy then just read that which is applicable.

I trust you find the insights helpful and that you, as I have found, experience the reward of people flourishing and performing highly under your leadership.

Attract, Create, and Keep Exceptional Employees

A great employee has two fundamental qualities – enthusiasm and teach-ability. The first denotes a passionate individual; the second signals someone who wants to develop and progress, is hungry to learn, and shows humility. If you find a third characteristic – highly developed skills – then you are really on to a winner. But even where skill levels are less than required, employees who have enthusiasm and teach-ability will rise to skill mastery much faster than those who don't demonstrate those qualities to begin with.

13 Key Points That Will Drive Positive Outcomes

1. 'Like attracts like'. If you have employees who absolutely love where they work, they will automatically boast about it to their friends. In turn, you will have people asking to work with you.

2. Look for enthusiasm and teach-ability when you recruit staff. If you identify them early, you are off to a flying start. Employees might have technical abilities but if they lack these traits there

is a high chance you will be helping them exit earlier. Much like trying to speed up a slow horse, trying to inject enthusiasm into a half-hearted, passionless person is virtually impossible.

3.   Provide clarity on your expectations. Give a potential team member a position description outlining roles, responsibilities and performance measures. Ideally, you should involve them in the process of establishing performance measures; this ensures a higher level of personal ownership.

4.   Provide ongoing feedback. Employees must know how they are progressing in their roles. Doing this in a formal annual per-formance review isn't enough. Create monthly feedback loops, so they know what they are doing well, and what they could be doing better. From many discussions with good employees and managers over the years, I know this is what they want most – almost without exception.

5.   Create a relational and fun culture. It shouldn't be a 'just do your job, head-down-tail-up' workplace. Provide an enjoyable environment where people can be themselves while achieving highly. This approach starts from the top down.

6.   Make a culture shift. Make your organisation one that focuses on results, not time.

7.   Work on yourself and your management team. Become excep-tional people developers and communicators, not just opera-tional 'doers'.

8. Show that you value your employees. They want to 'feel the love' not just the rod of correction. They want to know their contributions are highly valued.

9. Understand your organisation's purpose and vision. Communicate the message frequently to your people. Demonstrate how their daily work contributes to the bigger picture. Create advancement tracks, so they can develop their skills and passions, and make progress towards this greater vision.

10. Raise the performance bar. Set high targets and make it clear you will work with your people to achieve them, and hold them accountable for the results.

11. Treat your people like human beings. Recognise that work is just a part of their whole life. Don't view them, and communicate with them, purely as workers, as if they were one dimensional, and only good for 'doing the job'. Your best people will stay around longer if they are seen and treated as human beings.

12. Reward people appropriately. Make sure they are paid above award wages, wherever possible, and rewarded commensurately (not necessarily financially) for performance achievement.

13. Deal with toxic employees. Help them either to become healthy, or to exit the organisation. 'Infected' employees cause a high attrition rate among healthy team members. Good people want to work in a positive environment; they will leave if management does not address this toxicity.

This diagram represents some of the key points outlined above. If you get the drivers right and then add high managerial relational and communication skills, positive outcomes will be the by-product.

LONGEVITY AND PRODUCTIVITY ENHANCER

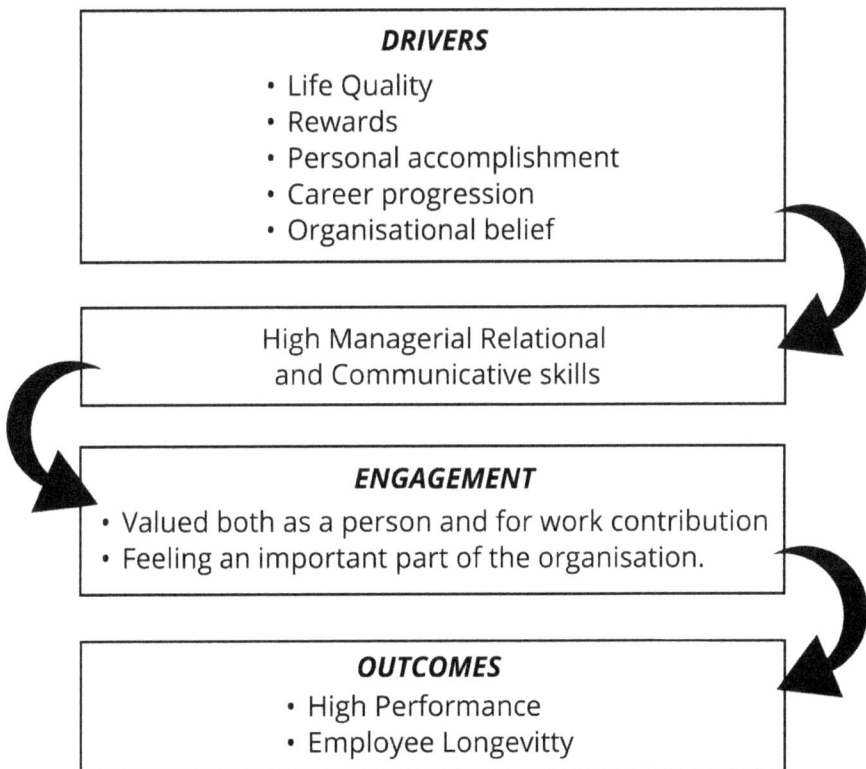

DRIVERS
- Life Quality
- Rewards
- Personal accomplishment
- Career progression
- Organisational belief

High Managerial Relational
and Communicative skills

ENGAGEMENT
- Valued both as a person and for work contribution
- Feeling an important part of the organisation.

OUTCOMES
- High Performance
- Employee Longevitty

Driver Components

Life Quality
- Job security
- Work-Life balance
- Personal needs taken into consideration
- Health and safety

Rewards
- Fair compensation
- Reputation and recognition
- Being a valued part of the organisation

Personal accomplishment
- Meaningful work tasks
- Empowerment and autonomy
- Sense of a job well done

Career Progression
- Education
- Mastery
- Promotion
- Clarity about improvement and advancement

Organisational Belief
- Belief in the future of the company
- Values
- Mission
- Vision

Understanding what our people need (the drivers) is the first step. The next is seeking to integrate these drivers into the workplace culture, through high relational and communicative skills. The result will be a more highly engaged and longer-term workforce. Many organisations fall at the second step. They might offer great benefits, but if they operate in a non-relational, officious manner and have poor communicative skills, employee engagement drops away – along with the expected positive outcomes.

Creating long-term employees, and a highly engaged workforce, doesn't just happen. It involves planning, implementation, and incremental integration into the cultural fabric of the organisation. Whatever your current experience – – whether you have high employee attrition or a highly satisfied workforce – you can construct a fresh vision of what your organisation could be.

2

Why Employees Quit

It has been said that employees don't leave an organisation – they leave management. This highlights the fact that those in leadership positions are largely responsible for attrition rates. External conditions, including family and personal reasons, financial considerations, or relocation to another city, might cause team members to move on, but internal organisational conditions contribute most to high rates of employee turnover.

All of us were created to progress, develop, and do something meaningful with our lives. Most employees want to know that their contributions in the workplace are making a difference. When this doesn't happen, they become unsettled. Concerns begin to surface, and if they are not addressed, employees soon begin to look for other options – employment that lets them make a meaningful contribution, and where their work is valued.

Over the years, I have spoken to countless employees, across many organisations, and here are some common reasons for resignations.

"I don't feel valued"

Many employees are not sure that they are doing a good job, or that their work is valued. They receive little, if any, praise for what they do, or recognition for extra effort. Management simply expects workers to get on with the job without feeling the need to be thanked or recognised.

"The managers are more interested in themselves"

Team members sense this a mile away. Where there is greater self-interest on the part of managers, as opposed to interest in the other, employees simply exist in an 'interest free' environment. While 'interest free' is great if you are buying furniture, in the workplace it is not conducive to people 'buying in' to the organisation. They might request something from management, suggest ideas, or provide exceptional work, but managers feel threatened because someone 'below' them might actually be more capable than they are.

"I can't progress as I would like to"

Often, employees want to make progress in their skills and careers, yet many organisations tend to slot people into positions, and feel satisfied that their organisational charts are complete. They fail to see that the charts should be dynamic, rather than static documents. As I mentioned earlier, all of us were born to grow and progress. To get a job in a static environment where we are not 'stretched', given recognition, or offered advancement can be debilitating. Yes, there are some who prefer simply to show up, do their jobs, and go home. The key for management, however, is to identify those who want to progress, and then to work with them to make it possible.

"My manager won't address key issues"

How many times have I heard this? Many managers are excellent peacekeepers, and won't allow the boat to be rocked at any cost. Sometimes,though, a boat needs to be sunk and a better one built instead.

I once worked with a company where the culture in the workshop was, frankly, negative. The main cause and contributor was the foreman. The business owner would not address the issue, instead allowing the foreman to do whatever he pleased – which included coming and going at will, taking breaks for as long as he wanted, and working at whatever pace he chose. The foreman, who was laziness personified, made the most of the situation. Because he was responsible for the other tradesman and the assistants, they followed suit. As you can imagine, productivity was very low.

Then a new tradesman joined the team. He started well – full of promise, and with a high work ethic – but within weeks, he acclimatised to the culture, and became just like the rest. After a number of months, he left the company.

The problem was the owner. He would not address the key issue – the foreman's performance. He chose to keep the peace rather than create conflict, and he paid the price for it: low productivity, financial loss, and the departure of a very able tradesman.

Eleven Exemplary Managerial Traits

Good managers:

1. Treat people as human beings, not merely workers. They communicate that they care about them personally, not just about their performance.

2. Create conflict if necessary, in order to obtain an outcome. They're not afraid to wade into it head on

3. Demonstrate openness to personal criticism, and seek ways to become more effective

4. Address employee concerns, no matter how trivial they might seem

5. Communicate the organisation's vision, and how each team member's work contributes to the broader perspective

6. Know how to create the sense of being a team, and bring individual workers into a collective team environment

7. Celebrate the wins

8. Create an enjoyable and fun culture to work in

9. Address key performance issues directly, and in private, with employees. Although many think this might create higher

8. attrition rates, it actually communicates value to individua employees, allowing them to know how they are performing.

9. Promote their teams above themselves

10. Understand their people – in terms of their strengths, weaknesses, and aspirations – and seek to provide the best opportunities for them to flourish within the organisation

11. Promote their teams above themselves

12. Understand their people – in terms of their strengths, weaknesses, and aspirations – and seek to provide the best opportunities for them to flourish within the organisation

Take Care Of Your Team

What managers often 'contribute' to workplace unhappiness and high staff turnover is, in fact, what they don't do. They simply don't care adequately for their people.

The best managers understand how to incorporate these 'care factors'.

Reasonable Workloads

Generally speaking, business owners are accustomed to paying a price to run a thriving enterprise. They know what it is to work eighteen hour days, seven days a week, when necessary. They know what it feels like to miss their loved ones at times, or to show up on holidays after the family has arrived, and they decline personal invitations to sporting events and social functions due to the high demands of the business. They also know this is part and parcel of running a successful business. The longer a business is established and the more people it employs, the more the owner can delegate tasks and the management of the organisation to other capable personnel. Eighteen-hour days can be reduced to twelve, then eight, and then none. For owners, the goal is to become redundant in the very business they initially established. Doing the hard yards comes with the territory, and while it is admirable, business owners, and highly motivated managers, often make the mistake of having the same expectations of everyone in the workforce. Management often equates hours worked with commitment. Therefore Jimmy, who is here before everyone else arrives, and then stays until 7pm every night, must be a more committed employee than Bob, who shows up and leaves according to his contractual requirements. As managers, do we tend to look only on the surface of things, equating hours with commitment, rather than at the quality and productivity of those hours?

I recently had a discussion with a tradesperson. He loved what he did, believed in the company's vision and values, and was highly motivated. But he was also weary.

"James (the owner) doesn't know when enough is enough. He keeps piling on jobs at the end of the day and we are expected to complete them prior to going home."

Here was an employee who, although he didn't mind working into the early evening occasionally, certainly did mind doing it consistently. And his physical and mental wellbeing was being affected. We subsequently called a meeting where the employee was able to verbalise his feelings about being overworked. The business owner, in turn, took the situation at face value, adjusted the job scheduling, and altered his own expectations to allow a more reasonable and 'sane' pace.

Clear Expectations

Some years ago I went into partnership with a colleague who knew what it was to pay the price to get a business up and running. He was one of the most astute business owners I have ever worked with. In the process of forming the partnership, he suggested that each of us create, and talk through, a list of what each of us expected from the other, prior to commencement. This was an excellent process, and both of us could return to the document whenever we felt there was any failure on the other's part. I am not suggesting you do this with every employee, but it highlights the fact that each person has a different set of expectations. The receptionist has expectations of the senior office administration manager, who in turn has expectations of the receptionist. Most of the time they are never clarified and worked through.

One the best clarification processes is a position statement, or job description, that contains roles, responsibilities and performance measures. Most position descriptions neglect performance measures, but having these are a powerful expectations communicative tool. Ideally, and wherever possible, employees should be involved in this process to more fully 'own' the performance measures.

When position descriptions – including performance measures – are in place, and employees fully embrace their position and expectations, the issue of overworking people is somewhat alleviated. If there is good documentation, and employees know that they can come to management at any time to discuss their position and its demands, happiness levels will rise, and attrition rates will go down. I have met many well-meaning employees who work long hours but are frustrated because management has failed to define what is actually expected of them. In the case of the tradesperson I mentioned earlier, I began to work with management to ascertain what performance measure (as in how many billable hours per day) would be satisfactory. If the employee met that measure then management could rest easy, knowing that they would reach their profit levels rather than driving their staff out of a fear of not knowing whether they were profitable. This approach demonstrates care for the employee.

Acknowledging Difference

Everyone is different. Some employees are driven to career success while others working beside them focus most of their energy on being with their families, and creating a loving supportive environment in the home. This is a case where 'different' just means different, rather than 'different' means wrong.

A critical mistake management sometimes makes is to treating all employees the same, rather than appreciating and honouring the fact that each is different from the rest. Some people, by their very nature, run at a slower pace than their faster counterparts. Some like to schedule and work briskly and methodically through their days, while others plod and plough from dawn to dusk (and beyond).

While on a consulting project with a company's senior management, I was working with a woman who was struggling with clinical depression. The business owner was smart enough to respect the healing process she had embarked upon and provided the flexibility for her to leave her desk and go for a walk whenever she needed to during the working day. It was a simple adjustment, but a clever one. The owner understood that each of his people was not only different, in terms of personality and behaviours, but also had individual histories and issues that they had to deal with from time to time. He had raised the bar high, expected a great deal, and clarified those expectations, but also treated each person as an individual.

The Essential 'Care Factors'

Avoiding overworking your employees, defining productivity measures and keeping employees accountable for them, and unfailingly factoring in the individual person, all show care for your employees – and that's very smart business.

In summary:

- Giving attention and care to employees is fundamental. Be aware that some employees do not want to be overworked and suffer for it, while others don't mind being pushed

- Focus on the quality of work, not the number of hours

- Set high standards and expectations

- Create a 'do what it takes' culture

- If someone starts to 'wobble', make sure you address the situation

- Treat every employee as an individual human being – a person not merely a worker

Make 'Yes' Really Mean Yes

One of the disappointments many of us face is being let down by people who say they will do something and subsequently fail to complete it. Their intentions are often honourable, but their follow-through is lacking. When it comes to management, one of the critical integrity factors is that when we say yes, it must really mean yes. Few things are as likely to create disintegration and mistrust as when leaders commit to do something and then subsequently fail to do it.

Countless times, in my consulting work, I have heard complaints from employees, managers, and executives, about peers and co-workers failing to follow through on what they had verbally committed to. Here are some examples:

> *"Bob tells us all not to be late to the weekly meeting, yet he often cancels it at last minute, doesn't show, or is late."*

> *"I repeatedly asked my manager for a meeting to discuss my work and my future. He always said he'd get back to me and never did, so I decided to leave the company."*

"Susan always agrees to what I recommend, and says she will do it, but rarely does."

"I continually have to chase my managers after the deadline, because they fail to complete their delegated tasks."

"James is a people pleaser. He says, and commits to, what people want to hear, and then goes and does his own thing."

"One of Melissa's performance measures is to have a report on my desk by 8am every Monday. She always agrees to it, but always has an excuse as to why it is late."

A verbal commitment with no subsequent action creates:

- Mistrust

- Non-engaged or disengaged workers

- Increased workplace attrition

- Dissension amongst management

- Low levels of performance and productivity

- Bypassing the 'commitment offender' in favour of more trustworthy people

'Failure to follow-through' Syndromes

Sometimes it's a case of 'When yes doesn't really mean yes'. I have noticed that there are three main syndromes associated with this failure to act on an agreed-upon task.

1.   The 'Take on everything' Syndrome

Motivation

People affected by this syndrome are often motivated by results. In order to continue performing highly in their role, they simply take on more and more work, to the point where they are consistently on overload. Their intentions are often well founded, but their delivery is lacking.

Antidote

Being clear on what is exactly expected of you in terms of roles, responsibilities and performance measures is essential. The other key is learning to say no. Say no to taking on things that are outside your sphere of responsibility. Say no to saying yes just so you can look good. Say no to living life on the edge. Step back, plan, work urgently but in a measured way, and drive for results. Let your yes really be yes.

2.   The 'Need to be loved' Syndrome

Motivation

In order to feel accepted, people who exhibit this syndrome commit verbally to complete tasks because they want to be accepted. Often they don't feel that who they are is acceptable; acceptance is based on what they do.

Antidote

This is often a case of seeking acceptance of others in order to gain self-acceptance. To be happy – in your self, and in your strengths and limitations – is the key. For some, the shift can happen in the shorter term; for others, depending on their history and the severity of the syndrome, it takes longer. Discussions with your colleagues or manager can assist in making the transition. Professional therapy often helps.

3.   The 'Keep the peace' Syndrome

Motivation

People who fall into this category dislike conflict. This motivates them to keep the peace at all costs.

Antidote

Learning to see that potentially creating external conflict (like saying no to a request that you know you cannot fulfil in the time frame) will create internal peace for you. Those who continually say yes and fail to deliver because they want to keep the peace simply create greater conflict in the long run.

Becoming a person of action and follow-through doesn't require much effort. It simply involves making a commitment to do what you say you are going to do. It is also about understanding why you have said yes, but failed to act in the past. Take the antidote for the syndrome that might apply to you, as suggested above, and make sure that your verbal yes results in follow-through, and really means yes.

5

Increase Productivity Through Communication

The verb 'communicate' means 'to make common'. Join, unite and participate in are also words that reflect this concept.

Human beings are essentially social beings, who thrive best when living in communities. Generally speaking, it is in communities that human beings are at their happiest and their most productive; this also applies to work communities.

In all my years (and they are quite a few) I have never come across a company or organisation that did not want its people to be productive. Some didn't particularly care for their employees' happiness but they certainly wanted productivity.

Productive workers generally display some of the following characteristics:

- They are more contented with themselves and their work

- They sense they have a 'calling' to what they are doing;

- They feel that their contributions are valued

- Their personal values and goals are aligned with the vision and mission of the organisation in which they work

Productivity has very little to do with personality, but everything to do with buy in or ownership. Productive workers are those who have 'bought in' to life and work, and who take personal ownership for the outcomes. They feel they are part of something important. Their motivation is intrinsic - it comes from within.

Non-productive workers, on the other hand, lack the characteristics described above. Some seek to be productive simply because they don't want to lose their jobs, but they do just enough to pass the mark, in order to collect their pay at week's end. They are motivated extrinsically – by the external rewards they receive for showing up and doing just enough, and no more.

Given these two fundamental elements of human beings – that we were 'born to belong' in communities, and that we are more productive when we take greater ownership and work toward something we believe in – it stands to reason that the workplace should provide for these needs. Communication is foundational in this.

Communication in the workplace needs to happen on three levels:

The Personal level

One of the major failings in management is to see employees purely as workers who are there to do a job, rather than as individual persons. Everyone who works in an organisation has life outside work, and life at work – but it is all one life. The expectation that our people should and disrespectful. The basis for communication and the building of a community is the idea that that all employees are individuals who need, and deserve, to be respected and appreciated - no matter how challenging they might be. To take an interest in people, not merely how they perform on the job is essential. The more people feel valued for themselves, the more their work will reflect this.

A business owner, whom I coached frequently, told me how highly he valued his senior office administrator. She (the administrator) asked me one day, "Am I doing a good job? I don't get any feedback". She is just one of the many employees that have asked me the same question over the years. While the owner highly valued the person and her contribution, he had neglected to communicate it to her personally.

Acknowledgement and feedback don't take much effort. It's easy to stop briefly, to look at someone, and to say "Thank you for what you do here. It really does make a difference".

The Team level

The larger the organisation the more challenging it is to retain the personal touch. In companies that are growing rapidly, many employees, at some point, feel left out of the loop as management struggles to keep up with the front and back end issues in the expanding organisation. This is where establishing separate teams, with team leadership, can be a useful strategy. In that way, all team members still receive the care, affirmation, and correction that they require on an ongoing basis.

The Group level

With advanced technology, keeping team members abreast of the latest developments is relatively easy. Group communication can be both under and over utilised. Some organisations rarely take advantage of it; a simple weekly update comprising last week's results, challenges, and wins is a useful way to start. On the other hand, some companies use electronic communication and neglect the personal touch. A manager who sends an email to the team member in the office next door, is missing the opportunity to have a personal communicative connection. Having a mix of both the personal and the written would serve organisations well.

Different People Hear Things Differently

As individuals, we hear things in different ways. How, for example, do people hear 'appreciation'? For some, it is through public praise; for another it's a small gift of recognition; for others it is conveyed with a meaningful 'thank you'.

A personal assistant, who worked with me for many years, was recognised for her contribution by the fact she could leave at midday every Friday. Along with words of affirmation, this small, individual weekly 'gift' showed gratitude, and provided her with a sense of belonging.

Understand your people, tailor your communication to them as individuals, and you will see increased levels of engagement and productivity as a result.

6

Be Flexible About Inflexibility

Running a business on your own can be a tough gig. Running a business with employees can be even tougher. And among the myriad of 'people challenges' you face, a major one is inflexibility.

"Bob is a great bloke but he's just inflexible. If I give him a new task or suggest a new way of doing things, he takes ages to make the shift, and often resists change. Susan, on the other hand, is fantastic. Drop a new task on her, and it's done immediately. Recommend a change, and after considering it momentarily, she just gets on with the implementation".

The inflexible and the flexible. The non-adaptive and the adaptive. As managers, we've all seen both.

If all employees were adaptive and flexible, life would be ideal. At ground level, though, we have reality!

A common failing in many of us is that we tend to judge others by our own personal beliefs and standards. We tend to approach life, situations, and people as if we hold the perfect truth, and anyone different from us is wrong. It seems to be the human default position - where different means wrong, as opposed to different just meaning different. If we could input 'flexibility' into an electronic process (and if the software were programmed to allow for that) the output would be guaranteed. Input – flexibility; output – flexibility. When we want to input 'change' into a human being, it's not that simple, yet many managers try to treat people like pieces of software. These attempts fail. Input – change; output – disappointment and frustration.

One of the greatest insights that I have gained – even though, as all of us would agree, applying what we learn is a different thing – is that every individual is different. We are not all programmed the same way. Like Susan, mentioned above, some have adaptive, flexible programming in their psyches. Bob, on the other hand is programmed for routine, stability, analysis, and reflection. Two very different individuals. Susan moves at a great speed and, although she accomplishes a lot, makes numerous mistakes. Bob moves more slowly, but makes fewer errors. Who is right, who is wrong? Who is better, who is worse? Should everyone be as flexible as Susan?

The approach I have taken in the businesses I have run, and in my current role as a management consultant, is that each individual is unique. Managers should work with others at an individual level, rather than treating a complete team in exactly the same way. It is important to understand the roles that each person is required to fill and what that role requires. An executive assistant (EA) needs to have similar traits to Susan. Bob as an EA would drive a CEO crazy. If I needed someone to fill the role of managing inventory, reporting, establishing and maintaining systems, Bob, with his inflexibility and thoroughness, would be ideally suited to this role. The mistake we make as owners and managers largely come down to this. We treat everyone the same; we treat every role the same; we expect everyone to do, and to be, the same.

In electronic programming this is acceptable, but in dealing with people it is not.

Is It Possible For People To Change?

Each of us has the ability to change, but it depends on the stretch required, and the individual's motivation for that change. Bob could become more flexible in his role, with proper coaching and support. But this change might only produce a 10% increase in flexibility. To expect him to change into a Susan is unrealistic. I wouldn't say impossible, but a lightning bolt would have to strike him in order for him to be reprogrammed to that extent. Highly unlikely. And to make Susan more like Bob? She would go crazy. Yes, we could help her slow down a little, and help her make fewer errors, but a shift of that magnitude is extremely unlikely.

Different just means different. Respect and work with your people as individuals. You will find that your team will flourish under these conditions.

7

Get It Right In Recruitment

It's a challenge that all businesses face – recruiting people who are well equipped for the specific roles and responsibilities they are required to take on. A related challenge is the even more onerous task of employing someone who is enthusiastic and teachable. Get it wrong at the start, and you'll pay for it further down the track. A common error made in the recruitment process is to focus almost exclusively on technical skills, where recruiters forget that each person in front of them is an assorted package of many other things. The right person for a role should certainly have capabilities based on technical expertise, but the personal package also includes:

- The right 'fit' with your organisational culture

- Enthusiasm and passion for the work

- Behavioural fit

- Teach-ability

- Personal goals and values

- Health considerations

- Family situation

A Suggested Recruitment Process

When working with companies, this is a process I use to ensure that the person selected is as close as possible to the ideal employee required for the role.

1. Establish a position description that identifies key areas such as roles, related responsibilities, and performance measures. You can find a free basic template titled: 'Position Description' at *http://www.rayhodge.com.au/category/templates-and-tools/*

2. Identify the type of person and behaviour that is best suited to the role. Examples might include:

   Administration Assistant – detailed and routine oriented

   Business Development Manager – fast paced, 'people person', with a level of detail orientation

   Receptionist – moderate paced, warm, 'people person'

Safety Officer – slower paced, analytical person with high attention to detail

3. Advertise the position, based on the details from the position description

4. Conduct an initial phone interview, based on the CV/resume that has been sent through

5. If you proceed to a personal interview, send out an application form. You can find a free 'Application for Employment' that I have created at http://www.rayhodge.com.au/category/templates-and-tools/

6. Conduct a personal interview. Once you know the candidates who can technically do the job, focus on understanding each 'person' in front of you. Intentionally sidetrack into their personal worlds. These sidetracks can provide you valuable information about potential new team members. Talk through their responses to the questions in the application form, and create more questions of your own, if relevant. Tell them that you value people being open about their challenges and failures. Disclosing something personal about yourself, and where you might have failed or felt challenged, can help them open up and be a little more transparent

7. Make sure to do background checks. Many bypass this step, and regret it later.

8.   Conducting a behavioural profiling exercise on the final selection of potential candidates can help to determine the behaviour required for the particular role, and then to ascertain the behavioural match of the person to that role.

Be proactive and assertive in the responses to your recruitment campaigns but take the time to work through the process thoroughly. Many employers simply 'grab' the first person that shows interest, if that person is technically adept. And to re-iterate: if you get it wrong at the start, you'll pay for it further down the track.

There's a 'whole' person that comes with those skills you are looking for.

How to Ascertain Enthusiasm and Teach-ability

1.   Enthusiasm

Here are some key questions to determine a candidate's enthusiasm:

- What's your dream job?

- Why are you applying for this position?

- What do love to do?

- What do you dislike?

- Where do you see yourself in 5 years' time?

- Tell me about a time in your current or previous work where you were intensely motivated?

- When have you been bored?

- What are the things you do that cause you to lose track of time?

- Why have you chosen this industry to work in?

Also find out

- What research has the candidate done on your company?

- Does this person display general enthusiasm and eagerness to learn and try new things?

The key here is to watch for those moments when the person lights up, or comes to life. This is often indicated by faster speech; 'over talking', can also indicate a subject a person is passionate about. The eyes light up, and body language is more animated. If you are dealing with a more 'analytic', as opposed to a more 'expressive', personal enthusiasm can be a little harder to gauge.

2.   Teach-ability

Here are some key questions to ask if you want to assess teach-ability.

- Tell me about what you have been learning, or reading.

- In which areas do you most feel you need to grow?

- If you were to be successful in this application, what areas do you think would present the most challenges?

- How would you deal with those challenges?

- Tell me about a time when you handled criticism or a constructive critique from your boss.

- Tell me about a time then you handled criticism or a constructive critique from your peers.

- What did you do in these situations?

- What did you learn from them?

- How do you stay up to date with developments in this industry?

Summary

I find that most employers interview and subsequently recruit based on technical abilities, largely neglecting the 'whole person' package. During interviews, it is important to take the time to understand the motivation, enthusiasm, and teach-ability of potential employees – not just their skills – because if you sacrifice this you risk employing the wrong person, and you will pay the price further down the track.

8

Gain your Employees' Trust

"The boss is an idiot."

"These are my rights."

"I wouldn't trust him at all."

"She's just looking out for herself."

"I get paid a pittance and look at him – driving around in his flash car." These are statements from employees that reflect mistrust and disillusionment.

In a business, the trust culture ranges from no trust in management (often resulting in both non-engaged and disengaged employees), right through to full trust, with high engagement and productivity, as shown in the graphic below.

TRUST CONTINUUM

Low   High

←————————————————————————————→

• Little or no faith/trust in management	→ Complete trust and faith in management
• Employee Status: Non Engaged/Disengaged	→ Employee Status: Highly Engaged
• Result: Low Productivity, Performance & Profitability	→ Result: High Productivity, Performance & Profitability

It All Starts With Management

Some time ago I consulted with two companies – both in the same industry, and in close proximity to each other. Company RST Pty Ltd was experiencing some of the following:

- High turnover of employees

- Challenges in employing good staff

- Internal Theft

- Infighting and employee disgruntlement

- Low profitability

- A culture of pessimism and mistrust

Company XYZ Pty Ltd, on the other hand, was experiencing:

- Long term tenure of staff

- Highly satisfied employees

- A culture of optimism and trust

- High productivity

- Reasonable profitability

Given that both companies were so similar, and existed within the same economic environment, it was exceedingly apparent that what I was observing outwardly, was a reflection on the companies' leadership. RST was led by someone who constantly complained about how hard things were, and about the idiots working for the company. The owner of XYZ demonstrated gratitude knowing that he could always hire good people, when necessary.

The outwardly visible results, in each case, were a direct reflection of the thinking, attitudes, and actions of the leader.

The Art Of Building Trust

Be Personable

The number one tip for management, when it comes to building trust is to be personable. It doesn't mean being someone's best buddy; it does mean being personally accessible.

Accessibility that builds trust comes in two forms.

1. Being physically present and available. Management from the shop floor will go further towards building trust, than management from behind a closed door. For employees to trust you as a manager, it is essential that they know they can approach you; they also need to see you at their level, engaging personally with them.

2. Being emotionally available. Many leaders are emotionally unavailable. They manage purely by meeting the company's goals, and the customers' requirements, and forget that the team they are working with are people (not merely workers). These people have lives outside work, different personalities, numerous motivations, personal standards and significant life challenges.

Good management is about being good with people, and essential traits of excellent leaders include the ability to understand their people, and be available - at the physical and emotional level.

<u>Be Interested</u>
As part of a consulting project I was engaged in, I had to deal with the conflict between a manager and his subordinate. The manager was emotionally disconnected – from himself and from others. He was all about systems and processes. His subordinate was a highly engaged people person; she needed to engage personally with others to give her work meaning and produce the required KPIs. Every Monday morning she would

ask him what he had done at the weekend. He said to me privately, "I don't give a f**k about the weekend; I just want her to do the job". He had no interest, no connection, and no personal care factor.

Take an interest in your people. Whether it's about their weekend, their families, or their hobbies, your simple expressions of interest build rapport and trust, and take you from a manager who is potentially distrusted or feared, to one whom team members will gladly trust and follow.

Raise the Bar
Here is a simple formula for building trust, based on increasing expectations.

1. Understand your people, and their skills, talents, goals, and ambitions.

2. Talk with them and define the next stage in their development and progress

3. Work with employees to reach the new bar height, and give them an ongoing honest critique along the way

This simple method communicates to employees that you value them, and consider them to be worthy of progression within the company. Your belief in them will build their self-belief and therefore increase their capacity to trust. Your honest appraisal of them along the way, and the knowledge that you are working beside them goes a long way to building highly performing individuals.

R.E.S.P.E.C.T

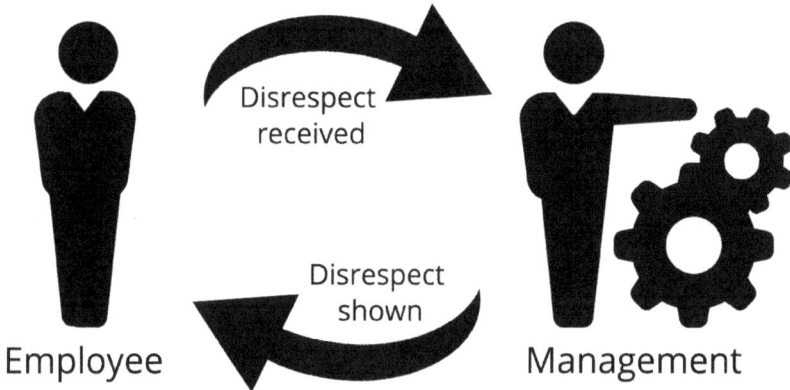

Running my own businesses in the past, and currently consulting with a range of organisations has led me to conclude that most managers and business owners are so absorbed in the fulfilment of their roles and responsibilities, and the meeting of performance goals that they can so easily put the people they lead in second place. Instead of viewing company growth as a team function, many managers narrow the focus and their approach tends to be individualistic, and devoid of team effort. This causes employees to feel the lack of care and respect and, in turn, creates a 'disrespect loop', as shown below.

We reap what we sow. Management that plants disrespect reaps disrespectful employees. The manager who demonstrates a lack for respect for the employee receives disrespect in return.

Disrespect Shown By Managers

Disrespect from management can be as simple as:

- Lack of acknowledgement for a job well done

- No interest in the 'person' – just treating the employee as a worker

- Saying "I'll get back to you" but continually failing to do so

- Not providing an ongoing critique, or performance reviews

- Failing to show up at team meetings, or continually cancelling them

- Failing to address advice from employees on what could be done better

Most people like to feel they are part of something bigger than themselves. When staff feel they are isolated individuals, performing their tasks with no recognition or possibility of advancement, they can end up feeling used, and certainly not respected.

One very skilled engineer, whom I know personally, continually went to her manager over a six-month period, asking to be considered for career advancement within the company. Her manager consistently said he would get back to her, but never did. She left the company. No respect shown by management resulted in disrespect from the worker. In another company, where I consulted, the mid level manager would always ask her senior manager how his weekend had been. He disliked this immensely, and would not engage in any personal conversation. The mid level manager was told she was there only to work and not engage in small talk. He planted the seeds of disrespect, which resulted in massive conflict between them. He reaped what he sowed, in this case, and it was not the harvest he wanted.

Another major cause of these feelings of disrespect in employees is managers not respecting differences. As people we tend to think that different means wrong, rather than different just means different. We tend to like people who are similar to us, and discount the rest, leaving them to get on with their work, and giving them less support. This is why some employees feel that the boss has favourites.

If, as leaders, we could see that different means different, and respect those differences in the people we lead, engagement levels would rise, and result in increased productivity.

Here is a classic scenario we find in the workplace.

Life Areas	Gary Vice President	Peter General Manager
Values	Career and Money	Family
Skills	Organisation	Organisation
Gifts and Talents	Finance	Strategy
Wisdom	Makes sense of conflicting views	Understands people intuitively
History	No loss in his life	Loss of a previous wife to cancer and child to suicide
Behaviours	Dominant	Stable/Steady
Personality	Extrovert	Introvert
Self Image	High	Low
Beliefs	Everyone should work as hard as he does	Results, not time, are what counts
Goals	To get to the top – no matter how	To be a loving provider for his family
Motivations	Expansive public perception	The personal well being and engagement of his team
Interests and Passions	Work	Coaching his son's soccer team

You will notice the significant differences between the two people described above. Time after time, I have encountered cases where someone like Gary judges those more like Peter for being slack in their work, despite the fact that they, like Peter, might demonstrate high productivity. We tend to judge the surface of things rather than look at concrete results.

In his book The 4-Hour Work Week, Tim Ferris speaks about his first job at an ice cream parlour, where he was hired for eight hours a day but completed the job in one hour. He worked smart not hard. After three days he was fired; the boss' parting comment was that perhaps, in the future, he would understand the importance of hard work. This is the classic case of one person judging another, based on his own standards, rather than seeing that different means different, not wrong, and honouring the fact that the 'different' person might have qualities that are worthwhile.

The comparison between Gary and Peter raises another issue that companies would do well to consider: the focus on outputs not inputs. Does it really matter that Peter meets or exceeds his performance criteria within the working day, rather than staying until 7pm, as Gary does every day?

Disrespect Shown By Employees

In cases where employees are just plain disrespectful, no matter how much managers care, the best solution is to deal with these situations directly.

What Can I Do Better?
Here is some language that might be useful:

"I might be wrong, but I get a sense from you that you don't like working here. The reason I say this is because I have noticed that [provide your observations and evidence]. Is there anything I can do to make things better for you?"

The key here is to get employees talking, to side with thema, and to be humble enough to admit to your own shortcomings as manager. Often when employees see that managers are willing to admit they could be doing things better, and will do what it takes to help their team members to be happy and productive in their work, the 'disrespect loop' is broken.

What If There's No Change?
No matter how much we care as managers, some people will not change. These people can be toxic to the culture of an organisation and need to be removed if their attitudes begin to affect other workers. I always suggest obtaining advice from legal sources, before effectively 'managing them out'.

The Mirror Effect

In conclusion, management sets the example. Our workplace cultures are a direct reflection of the company's management. If we see people as important, valuable assets to our business, and if we treat them accordingly, then the culture will be one of respect and vitality. If, on the other hand, we see people purely as a 'necessary evil' and that life would be better without them, they will feel that perception and respond accordingly.

10

Motivate Your People

The word 'motivation' comes from the Latin verb movere (to move). The Oxford dictionary states that it is the factor *"causing or being the reason for something"*.

One of the highest challenges for management and business owners is that of having their employees working somewhere near full capacity – whether from a time perspective (ensuring that they are productive for the majority of their working days) or in terms of the individual's talents and skills. In short, employees are doing what they love to do (with passion), working in a role that is suited to them (with the appropriate skill set) and working productively (with effective use of time).

Intrinsic Verses Extrinsic Motivation

Intrinsic motivation is best described as the motivation that comes from within a person. Intrinsic motivation is all about doing what we find enjoyable and are passionate about, which relates to what we value highly and from which we gain a personal sense of satisfaction.

Extrinsic motivation is that which comes from outside the person. Extrinsic motivation is about external factors that create the stimulus to achieve or perform certain tasks. An example of this is when children do what they are told, because of the potential rewards, if they do, and negative consequences, if they don't. Or when an employee is told she is free to leave the company if she doesn't jump on board; or where people are rewarded with time off, or with financial and other material perks.

Both intrinsic and extrinsic motivators have their place, but it is my view that those who are motivated from within will perform at higher levels for a lot longer than those who expect or receive external rewards.

Enthusiasm

In the workplace, the starting point is the hiring process. Identifying keenness and passion for work (enthusiasm) should be primary; gauging skill levels secondary. It is much easier to train people in the technical aspects of the job than to teach them to love their work. The latter is akin to trying to make a slow horse speed up: it just doesn't happen. Many employers ignore this important distinction. When we experience labour shortages or production demands, and we don't really understand the whole person, we tend to hire anyone that is, technically, somewhere near the mark, rather than pursue someone with enthusiasm.

Internal Drivers

One of the key observations to consider when both hiring and working with people is that all of us are motivated by what is most important to us. If we value money, and the freedom it brings, then money is the motivator. If satisfaction from a job well done is important, then that is reward enough. If we prize time with the family, then that will be what drives us. Our workers are no different. Different factors drive different individuals according to what is most important for them. Tap into these internal drivers, adapt the workplace to accommodate them, and you will have employees more inclined to be intrinsically motivated in their work. Their work will then relate to their higher values, and both they and the company will reap the rewards.

Skill Sets and Role Alignment

I have worked with numbers of employees and managers over the years who, when I began coaching them, were trundling along, doing what they had to in order to keep their jobs, but doing little more than that. After I worked with them to identify their natural talents and skill sets (and I've found that enthusiasm is linked to these), and then, in accordance with senior management, either move them into more suitable roles or redefine their current roles, their motivation and subsequent productivity increased dramatically.

Purpose

All of us, including the people who work for us, are designed to contribute something to the world, and need to feel that what we are doing daily is of value. To help our employees link their daily work to a purpose is to give them a powerful intrinsic motivator. One person's purpose might simply be to provide for a family and raise children in a loving environment. Another person might be driven to free children from sex slavery in Cambodia. Taking the time to understand our employees' greater purposes, and to demonstrate our interest, and belief in them will go a long way towards creating an engaged and highly performing staff. Another key point is to help your team to see the greater reason, or purpose for the business itself. You've no doubt heard the story of The Three Bricklayers. When the first one was asked what he was doing, he simply stated the task outlined for him: "I'm laying bricks". The second, when asked the same question, said, "I'm putting up a wall". The final bricklayer declared proudly "I'm building a cathedral".

What is your cathedral? What is the greater purpose for your company? If you can unravel this, and then instil it into the fabric of your organisation, it will help a greater number of team members jump on board with you as you go. It will also encourage the 'wrong' type of people to jump off.

Money As A Motivator

I have heard many business owners and managers lamenting the poor motivation and low-level performances of their teams. The discussion invariably gets around to creating a bonus structure, to lift the motivation of the workforce. My question to them is always this: "What if they are not motivated by money?"

In a previous business, I had a staff member who knew money was important, but an extra long weekend to be with her family was a higher motivator. I structured her role and performance criteria to allow her to leave at midday every Friday. She stayed with me for years. I also had an account manager who worked from home, as he was the principal carer for his children. I structured his work around this primary purpose and also gave him complete autonomy. I took away the need for him to work a certain number hours per week, and created instead a results-based position. His motivation and performance were far greater than if I had thrown more money at him.

Incentivise everyone with financial rewards and you could potentially miss the mark much of the time. As Edward L Deci observed:

> "If a person who is intrinsically motivated to perform an activity begins to receive external reinforcement for the activity, what will happen to his intrinsic motivation? Previous studies and the present study indicate that money decreases intrinsic motivation, while verbal reinforcements tend to enhance intrinsic motivation".[1]

There is nothing wrong with financial incentives, but if you head down this path, also consider incentives based on what drives the individual, and think about rewarding team performance rather than just individual effort.

---

[1] Edward L Deci – Journal of Personality and Social Psychology 1972, Vol. 22, No. 1, 113-120

Motivate Your People
Shift From Mediocrity to High Performance

Business owners and managers are often faced with the challenge of extracting high performance from employees who are happy with mediocrity. This becomes particularly apparent when position descriptions, complete with roles, responsibilities and performance measures are handed, in their entirety, to employees. More often than not, employees will manage a compliant nod of agreement, return to their tasks, and desperately hope that the performance measures outlined were really just an afterthought and that their performance won't be measured at all.

Here is an example:

Role: Account Manager for the Western region

Responsibilities:

- Make monthly onsite visits to all current A grade customers, bi-monthly visits to B category customers, and quarterly calls to all others

- Increase number of new accounts

- Increase number of products per customer

Performance Measures:

- Customer complaints to be less than 1%

- New accounts must increase by10% p.a.

- Current GP percentage maintained

- Number of products per customer to increase to 2.4

Management should have high expectations, there's no doubt. It is quite another thing for the Account Manager in this case to 'own' what is expected of him. When performance measures are handed down from the top, without a consultative process with the employee, there often exists a gap between management's expectations and the employee's internal motivation to meet them.

If this gap currently exists in your organisation, consider following through on these:

- With your employees, work through the position description and your expectations, emphasising the fact that they are an important part of the organisation, and that their input is crucial to the ongoing success of their particular departments (unless of course this isn't the case.)

- Ascertain the key challenges they face in meeting the standards

- Understand what drives them, and tailor the conversation accordingly a

- Be prepared to lower the bar (in certain cases) and raise it in others

- Work towards having employees fully accept and own the expectations. Whether it takes one meeting or six – do it!

- Conduct performance management during the next 90 days, with weekly meetings and relevant reports

- If they can't make the shift away from mediocrity, then perhaps there is a more suitable department (or other company) for them. The goal is 100% ownership on both sides. Management sets the bar high; the employee fully embraces the expectations.

Put The Right People In The Right Places

Can you create a team that actually wants to be at work?

Clearly some managers can, and others haven't yet achieved it.

"I couldn't do it without the people we have at this place", I hear one manager say. "I am blessed with a great team".

'My life would be so much easier if I didn't have to employ these (expletives deleted)s", a business owner emphatically states.

People. They are a rich source of fulfilment for one manager, and the bane of another's existence. Roses on the stem of the company structure? Or the thorns that prick the sides of our daily existence? Which is true for you?

In his book Good to Great, Jim Collins speaks of the importance of getting the right people on the bus and the wrong people off it. When there's a team, all wanting to go in the same direction, and sharing common goals, ideals and standards, it makes for a great ride. The bus might not always go in the direction anticipated, but when the passengers can maintain their own high standards and morale they will happily journey to to wherever is best for the group as a whole. On the other hand, a mixed busload of individuals, each absorbed by self-centred interests, lacking focus, passion and motivation for the common good, will make for a long and miserable journey, for bus driver, business owner or manager.

Take the 'people challenge'

When you consider that you are at work for about one third of any working week, having the right people around you not only makes sense from a business performance perspective, but also in terms of the personal satisfaction you take in your work.

What I consistently find, in meetings with business owners (and in the occasional 'meeting' with myself) is that we are all very good at pointing the finger outward at others, rather than back toward ourselves. We are happy to blame others, but neglect to look in the mirror and realise that the quality of the people we have on board is a direct reflection of our people and management skills.

The other key thing is that some business owners tire of the 'people challenge' and simply choose to live with the situation rather than continually work at changing the culture and individual behaviour and attitudes. "Better the devil you know than the one you don't" is the mantra of some business owners. This attitude can create a disempowering work environment.

It is challenging enough to run your own business, and deal with the million things that are constantly on your plate without having disgruntled employees with whom you have to share a large part of your life.

Here is a list of the most common 'people issues' I encounter while working with companies:

- Poor attitude

- Sloppy workmanship

- Low performance and productivity

- Individualism: no team collaboration

- Clocking on and off 'to the minute'

- Unwillingness to give extra, unless paid overtime

- External motivation (company policy, or accountability) rather than self-motivation

- Doing just enough to keep the job

- Lack of detail and care where required

- Dislike for change

- Inability to think independently

I'm sure you can add to this list, but you can see from this snapshot that the people issue can be a major challenge and, unless we are pro-active, in taking steps to change the situation, things will obviously stay the same. As the well-worn statements remind us: *"If you do what you've always done, you'll get what you've always got"* and *"The definition of insanity is doing the same thing and expecting a different result"*

Start with what you have

Most of us already have a team around us. It might be one we have chosen, or inherited, or a mixture of both. Whether it numbers two, two hundred, or two thousand, it is a team of people who are part of our working world. And just as it is important to understand our current position, before we start any improvements in processes, the same is true when working with people. We need to evaluate those we have on board.

One of my observations is that healthy work places are those where business owners, HR and departmental managers tap into the sources of internal motivation in their people. Each of our employees has dreams, goals and motivations, some related to work, some to external pursuits. The smart manager or business owner takes time to understand these internal drivers and helps their people align their activities accordingly. Here are a few areas to start with:

Passion

Some time back I worked in a church environment, building teams of volunteers for various events and productions. My role was to gather good people, and to create professional performances and productions. I had to work with people who were already working full time in other jobs. A challenge to say the least!

One of the things I quickly learned was that I didn't have the luxury of offering people more pay. In fact there was no financial leverage I could use. I had to tap into something quite different.

I discovered very early that the people that ended up on my team were passionate people. They worked at their daytime jobs and then came to night time rehearsals and completed weekend tasks because they loved-what we were doing. I realised that if I took the time to understand who they were, in the context of their motivations, I could direct them into roles and functions that they were happy to take on. Just this one insight brought many gifted and talented people our way. They wanted to do something more than their day-to-day work. For weeks prior to our Christmas performances, they would come after work for night time rehearsals – because they wanted to, not because of any financial reward. They wanted to feel that they could contribute to something bigger and use their gifts and talents in a personally satisfying way.

Creativity

Bob performs an administration role within the company, but he has a wide creative streak in him. Shirley, the business owner, has observed this – in their discussions and in the way he generates new ideas for the business. She has continued to nurture Bob's creativity, giving him the space and freedom to try out different things. Sometimes his ideas don't work, but more often than not they hit the mark. Bob is now much happier than when his former manager boxed him into his role.

Leadership

Brad is a fourth year apprentice who is good at his trade. He also seems to show an aptitude for leading people. Upon observation onsite and in the workshop, John, his divisional manager, has noticed that he often organises tasks and people. Amazingly, the others are happy to follow his lead and direction. From this observation, John sits him down and asks about what drives him. His response is: "I like my trade and the satisfaction of a job well done, but for some reason I get greater satisfaction from seeing the other crew members happy in their work. I don't deliberately try to organise them but for some reason they keep asking me for direction and, to be honest, even though I feel out of my depth at times, it seems to work and I really enjoy that aspect of my job".

Volunteering

Kylie works in accounts but every Monday she talks about how great her weekend was, because of the volunteer work she does. Joanne, the CEO observes this drive and asks Kylie whether she would be interested in helping their organisation become more involved in giving back to the community. Kylie obviously responds positively to this, and one of the notable changes that Joanne sees in her is increased motivation in her regular role.

In these examples, the workers had something else driving them, and the astute business owner or manager tapped into it and continued to direct them in the context of their particular motivations. They didn't try to motivate them, they simply observed what was happening and, in a sense, unharnessed the workers, allowing them to explore more fully and run with the motivation.

Understanding our people, in terms of what drives them internally is a key to creating long term, satisfied employees and managers. Merely keeping them accountable to a job description doesn't achieve this end.

Understand people's values

People are motivated towards what they value most. Similarly, they cannot be motivated towards what they don't value. In my own staff, and from observations made in other businesses, I have encountered many things that people value. Some of them are: Standards of excellence – in their workmanship

- Freedom and ease – they like to have time off

- Money

- Partying on the weekend (every day for some)

- The welfare of others

- Health

- Family

- Education

There are obviously many others, but this sample is an indicator of some of the values that motivate our people. We all live our lives according to what we value highly, or otherwise. Understanding what our employees value helps us create a happy workforce.

I often am asked whether or not incentivising all staff with financial bonuses is a good idea. My answer is this: when we look into what people value most, it's clear that some would prefer extra time off, some would like a gym membership, and others want to be involved in helping the community. So yes, paying our people well prevents them looking for more highly paid work elsewhere, which in itself is a good thing, but thinking that only offering more money will keep our good people is erroneous.

I have worked with a number of people who respond better to to additional time off than to extra money. Some want financial bonuses attached to performance, while others who value career advancement prefer ongoing education. Each person has a set of different areas that they deem to be important to them. When we tap into them, workers understand that they are important to our business. They see that we are interested in them as people and, wherever possible, we will tailor our business model according to what is important to them.

One thing to note: Business owners and managers often say, "I don't have the time to spend understanding my employees in this way". My observation is that management will spend the time either creating a happier workplace or constantly recruiting because of higher staff turnover. Spending time with your current people yields greater long-term results in terms of productivity, profitability, creativity, and employee satisfaction.

This is the key to building a workforce that is more likely to stay for the longer term. It lets them know that it isn't all about making more money for the boss, but that the boss is actually interested in them. A big difference!

Behaviour

When I talk about behaviour here, I am not talking about good and bad, or right and wrong. I mean the behaviour that demonstrates who people really are, in the context of the environment in which they find themselves. As you would be aware, our behaviour changes and adapts to the different environments we are exposed to. Think about your own actions for a moment. When you are at work, you demonstrate behaviours that are different from to those you might express at a party, or when you are at home at the weekend. We don't 'try' to behave in certain ways; these are natural expressions.

Some broad types of behavioural expressions are:

- People-oriented

- Task-oriented

- Faster-paced

- Moderately-paced

- Expressive

- Passive

- Accepting

- Assessing

- Driven

- Detail-oriented

These are quite general terms, but if you review your workforce (and yourself for that matter), you will see some of these types of behaviours quite clearly demonstrated.

One of the models I have used in many situations, to help understand 'who's who in the zoo' is the DiSC Behavioural Profiling model – a profiling system that helps people understand themselves. For managers and business owners, it gives insight into those they have on board. It can also be used to clarify particular types of behaviours required for certain roles within the company.

One of the powerful uses of this kind of profiling tool (and there are many others available on the market) is that it helps us understand behaviour as a neutral expression of a person's 'way', rather than, as I said earlier, seeing behaviour as 'right or wrong'.

Here are some examples:

1. James, one of your tradesmen, constantly neglects to complete his job card in full detail. He leaves out parts he has used, and gives a summary of the job, rather than a detailed explanation. This causes continual frustration for the administrative staff when they try to convert the job card into invoicing format.

    The interesting thing about James is that your customers give fantastic feedback about what a 'great guy he was'; they refer your business to their friends due to his 'likeability'. You also notice that   he seems to love life, jokes continually, and is great with people in general. The other thing you notice is that his productivity is very high; he completes tasks very quickly, al-though the number of warranty callbacks is also quite high.

When we look at this in terms of behaviour, we can quickly gain insight into James' behavioural strengths and weaknesses, as they pertain to his particular role.

Strengths

- People oriented; quite accepting of others

- Faster paced

- Influencer

Weaknesses

- Low on detail

- Works too fast at times; many callbacks

2. Sarah has recently been employed in your business as a general manger. She came to you through a recommendation from a colleague, and her CV was quite impressive. Forty percent of her role, however, is to market your business, as you needed someone to fill both roles in the short term. As things progress, you find she is great at detailed analysis, strategic planning and direction, and providing all kinds of charts and reports, but the marketing seems to get left until last, and doesn't quite happen the way you envisage. You also notice that the divisional managers don't warm to her; her straight-talking delivery of facts and instructions tends to rub people up the wrong way. You want someone who can get out there and pursue new customers, as well as manage the business. You don't want her to sit in her office all day, which she tends to do.

Some behavioural observations as they pertain to Sarah's role:

Strengths

- Detail-oriented

- Moderately paced

- Task-focused

Weaknesses

- Lack of people orientation

- Bluntness (indicating task not people orientation)

- Over analysis

This model uses employee strengths and weaknesses to position our people in the right roles. It also helps us to work with those in current roles (like the two above) – to promote their strengths and work more objectively with their weaknesses.

This type of behavioural profiling works well, because it helps us to be objective during the process. Often I hear business owners and managers bemoaning the fact that a team member is slow, sloppy, brash, or talks too much. When we look at these apparent weaknesses in the light of the fact that people are wired in certain ways, and in combination with their particular environment, we are better able to work with people from a rational standpoint.

Consider the examples above.

Knowing that James is great with people, but not so good on detail, gives us something tangible to work with. A detailed job card is essential for right pricing, invoicing, and high customer satisfaction; it also keeps the administration out of the frustration zone.

Armed with this understanding, we can train James to take more time to complete job cards, and ensure he does them after each job. Because of the high number of recalls, we can teach him to go back at the end of each job and check all work against what was meant to be completed, and to ensure all is working correctly. This shows the customer that everything is done according to what was requested.

Change doesn't happen overnight but, given time, and persistent training, James' areas of weakness can be improved to a satisfactory level. He will probably never get to the level of some of the other tradesmen, in terms of detail on his job cards, but it will be enough to promote accurate invoicing, so as not to lose you money.

Sarah's case is clearly one of role and behaviour mismatch. She is obviously very gifted in administration, reporting and analysis, but lacking in people skills. Often, avoidance of an aspect of one's role can be a good behavioural indicator. In her case, never getting to the marketing tasks indicates high task and detail orientation to administration, and low people orientation in terms of marketing. Obviously, this is an over-simplified explanation but is, nevertheless, a significant indicator.

Having taken Sarah through the profiling exercise and gained some understanding of her dominant behaviours, we might choose to:

1. Change her role, so that she is solely focused on the analysis side of her job, and employ a part time marketing person, or

2.   Work with her closely and make her more accountable for fulfilling her marketing role, questioning her more deeply as to why she isn't getting to the marketing tasks.

I have found, in over twenty years of working in this area, that people are best employed in their areas of strength. There is only a certain amount of 'stretch' that someone can manage, in the attempt to strengthen an area of weakness. Often this is totally frustrating for the person involved. In Sarah's case, if the second option were chosen, her gains in the people and marketing area might be minimal, given her detail and task orientation.
It has been shown that the most successful people build on their strengths, and outsource or employ to compensate for their weaknesses. Having an understanding of the various roles and job requirements within your business, and understanding yourself and team members in this light, will help you get the right people in the right places, and the wrong people out their 'mismatches'.

Nurture your people

Let's think about gardens for a moment. Healthy gardens don't just happen. You can have two properties side by side in the same street, each receiving the same amount of sunshine and rain; one is abundant and the other… well, more on the scraggly side of things. What's the difference? Nurture.

A garden needs to be nurtured if we want it to be lush, ordered, and pleasing to the eye. If we want to have team members that are focused, growing, and all on the same side, they have to be nurtured, too. This is a challenge for many business owners and managers.

We've already looked at starting with where you are, and the importance of getting to know your people, in terms of what they are passionate about, what their highest values are, and their individual behavioural style. Armed with that information, let's look at how we can nurture them, from where they are right now.

The Traits Matrix

This is a simple tool I developed for the purpose of identifying the strengths and weaknesses of your people, in relation to the company's values and standards.

First, make up a list of the values and standards that your company stands for. It might include enthusiasm, passion, excellence, teamwork, teachability, and discipline. After you have a list of these ideal qualities, put them into a matrix, with your employees' names in the left hand column, and the traits along the top row. Then, place a tick in the relevant cell if the employees currently display that quality, and a cross if they don't. You can use a number or percentage system if that works better for you.

You now have a matrix that gives you greater insight into your team, and shows where the weak areas are. It also enables you to plan the specific type of training your people need. When recruiting, be aware of these qualities (and weak areas) and design your application and interview questions accordingly. This way you can nurture your people, and create a healthy workplace.

Here is a sample matrix:

Name	Enthusiasm	Team work	Discipline	Teachability	Conflict resolution
Bob Smith	✓	✓	x	✓	✓
Karen Jones	x	x	✓	x	✓

A template is available at: http://www.rayhodge.com.au/category/templates-and-tools/

You can also build on this model to incorporate your own observations of the individual's passion, values and behaviour. The advantage of having all this information on one page is that you can:

1. Clearly see who is on your team

2. Identify what particular focus is needed for each individual

3. Gain clarity about mismatches between people and their roles

4. Plan training and specific coaching, according to areas of need

5. See who is progressing and who is stagnating

6. Identify who should stay and who might be better placed elsewhere

Raising the bar

I recently read the story of Stephen Bradbury, the speed skater, who won gold at the 2002 Salt Lake City Winter Olympics. In his autobiography he said that he had always wanted to be a gold medal winner for Australia; he eventually achieved it, even though it was in the most unlikely circumstances. He devoted his whole life to continuous improvement. He had set the bar, and he wasn't content until he jumped over it (or skated through it, in his case). Compare him with someone who is simply happy to improve to the point where she can skate and not fall over. Two vastly different settings for that bar! As Henry Ford once said: "Whether you think you can or can't – you're right".

In terms of our business, and our people, the height of the bar determines how far they will rise. If we are content with the 'devil we know', then mediocrity will be the height people settle for. If excellence, passion, superior customer experience, fine workmanship, minimal error rates, high productivity and profit are our goals, and if we communicate them continually to our teams, and constantly monitor and nurture each individual, then guess what? Our employees will more likely rise to the height we set. And what's more, the people who are happy simply to skate for pleasure, rather than win gold medals, will gradually move off to other skating rinks.

13

Are Your People Leading You?

I have met many leaders in my time who, instead of leading their employees, have inadvertently handed over the leadership reins to them. Instead of the leader grasping their vision for the future, owning the vision, communicating it, and leading their people into the future, they succumb to being followers of their own employees. They would rarely admit it but it frequently plays out in reality.

Here are some sample scenarios:

- The leader suggests to a staff member that, in order to save time, she should change the way she does things. The staff member starts to sulk and, not wanting to offend, the leader yields to the employee.

- A team member tells the boss the conditions of his employment. The leader knows it's not in the best interest of the company but, for fear of losing this person, gives in

- A foreman runs his own show in the workshop. He takes breaks whenever he wants to, goes at his own pace, and disregards the performance measures placed upon him. He knows his manager won't sack him, because he is the 'best' in the industry.

Fear is often the underlying reason why management continually yield to their staff. It might be fear of hurting the person; fear of not being 'mates', as you've always been; fear of conflict; fear of being seen as less than you want to be; or fear of losing the employee.

If you allow your people to lead, and do as they please, you will go round in circles. Leadership is about leading not following. Know where you are headed, and lead your people there. If they don't like it, work with them to get them on board. If they won't, let them go. Some employees are like kids who have always had their own way. If something isn't to their liking they sulk or sabotage. Point this out to them and if the behaviour persists, help them leave. Better to lead fifty people working at 100% capacity, than one hundred working at 50%. Your life will be easier, your people happier, and your business healthier.

14

Tough Love Leadership

Tough Love Leadership is a style of leading that was demonstrated by one of my best clients. He was tough when he needed to be, but also gave enough love for people to feel valued. His management team was highly engaged – a direct reflection of his leadership.

Here is a list of traits he exemplified, and which are well worth emulating:

1. He **places value** on his people and their contributions – and they know it

2. He has **personal knowledge** of his people – and takes time to get to know them individually.

3. He understands **role placement** – and people are therefore positioned according to their strengths and passions

4. He **raises the bar** to achieve high standards

5. He sets **targets and KPIs** that everyone is aware of

6. He **works with, and supports his team** in achieving those targets.

7. He **holds people accountable** for results.

8. His **abundance mentality** allows him to release people who need to leave. He is not held captive by those who think they are indispensable.

9. He manages people to **go up or out**; staying still is not an option

10. He is **focused and measured.**

11. He **lives up to his word** and demonstrates consistency

12. He always **gives credit** where credit is due

13. He **rewards** his people

14. He **allows for autonomy** in an environment of trust

15. He uses **collaborative leadership** – not an autocratic style

16. He **leads from the floor** – not from behind a closed door

High Engagement = High Performance

The Massage Therapist

Upon turning the big five zero, I decided to treat myself to a massage. As the therapist was doing her work on me I asked: "What is the worst thing about your job?" She sheepishly responded, "When men ask for sexual massages". I thought, "Well that's good, and my partner will certainly appreciate that." Then I asked: "What do you love about your job?" "The money", was her firm response.

Conclusion: Non-Engaged

The Foreman Wore Slippers

I was consulting with a company that had issues with its workshop staff. They were managed by a supervisor who worked in his slippers, came and went as he wanted – often disappearing for days on end without notice – and demonstrated total disregard for job timeframes. The quality of work was dismal. I could go on. The other tradesman and assistants followed his lead.

Conclusion: Actively Disengaged

The Industrial Management Team

Another industrial company I worked with had an assertive leader, who valued his people, supported them immensely, and raised the performance bar high. When I interviewed the management team, they all spoke highly of the owner, were keen to continue in their quest to improve company performance, and willing to work on their own personal development.

Conclusion: Engaged

The Terms Defined

Engaged: These individuals choose to give their best. They make positive contributions and are emotionally committed to the vision, values and goals of the organisation.

Non-Engaged: They have low levels of motivation, and average performance in their work. They do just enough to get by.

Actively Disengaged: These individuals communicate, through words, attitude or body language, that they are unhappy in their work. They demonstrate a disregard for management and other workers, and are most likely to stir up dissension and negativity among co-workers.

What The Stats Say

The much touted workplace engagement study from Gallup Research, published in 2013, revealed the following statistics for Australia:

- Only 24% of all workers are engaged in their jobs (second to the US, where engagement levels are 29%)

- 60% of workers are not engaged

- 16% of employees are actively disengaged

- Engagement levels in leadership positions were rated at 19%, compared with employees, at 24%

Indicators Of Engaged Individuals

- Enthusiastic and energetic

- Performance watching, not clock watching

- Prepared to go above and beyond what is expected of them

- Creative and Innovative

- Seeking to excel in all that they do

- Willing to try new things, and prepared to fail occasionally

- Choosing to love their work

- Accepting personal responsibility

- Taking sick days only when they need to

- Showing transparency

- Owning up to mistakes

- Demonstrating loyalty

- Willing to learn and grow, both personally and in their job

Indicators Of Non Engaged Individuals

- Showing little enthusiasm, with no additional contribution

- Clock watching

- Putting up with the job

- Lacking desire to be better in their work

- Simply doing the job, collecting their pay, and going home

Indicators Of Actively Disengaged Individuals

In addition to being the opposite of the engaged types, these individuals wilfully express the following traits and actions:

- Obstinacy

- Disregard for management and directives

- Loving themselves more than their jobs and colleagues

- Promoting themselves as powerful, when in fact they are not

- Purposefully creating dissension and negativity

Benefits Of Highly Engaged Workplaces

- Greater innovation in the market place

- Higher levels of staff satisfaction, with increased productivity

- Enhanced quality and workmanship, and fewer errors

- Higher sales and profitability

- Lower attrition rates, leading to lower recruitment costs

- Higher levels of customer satisfaction and loyalty

Other research on this subject shows that:

- Companies with low engagement scores earn 32.7% less operating income than companies with more engaged employees

- Engaged companies outperform competitors by as much as 28% overall

- Engaged companies grow profits up to three times faster than their competitors

- Highly engaged employees are 87% less likely to leave the organisation

- Engaged companies have double the level of customer loyalty

- Engaged companies have double the level of productivity

How To Increase Engagement Levels

Improve Life Engagement
When thinking about how to help non-engaged or disengaged employees reach high levels of engagement, we should look at them (and ourselves for that matter) as individuals, and determine whether they are, in fact, engaged in life itself.

- What are their interests outside work?

- What do they do when they are not at work?

- Do they have quality, loving relationships?

- What do they talk about most? Family, travel, spirituality, community service, wealth, hobbies?

Answers to these questions give insight into what their primary values are.

Full engagement in the workplace starts with life engagement. Many people, even those in their thirties and forties, have already 'died'. They have given up learning, growing, and loving, and are content to meander through life till they pass on to the next world.

As Ashley Montagu wisely said: "Die young as late as possible".

Have a Dream

Think back to when you were a child. What were the things you dreamed about? As we grow up the dreams we once entertained are often knocked out of us. Instead we hear: "Who do you think you are?" "You're hopeless at doing that." "You won't amount to anything." Combine these with repeated failures, redundancies, financial and relational difficulties, and life can end up being just too hard.

People who retain passion, curiosity, a dream, a cause, or a purpose (or willingly pursue these if they disappear), perform better than those who feel they are stuck in a holding pattern until they die.

We all have the opportunity to create a great life, but sometimes we give up, stop trying and 'die young'. The key is to go back to your dreams – or to start dreaming again.

- What do you want to do?

- Who do you want to be?

- What do you want to be remembered for?

- Where do you want to go?

- What new skills do you want to learn?

- What are you curious about?

Align Passion and Skills

Understanding ourselves in the context of the talents and skills we possess helps us find the type of work that will keep us fully engaged in our careers. Many people settle for second best. For example: an extremely gifted communicator and influencer ends up settling for a data entry role; a strategic thinker and planner accepts a sales job. These normally highly engaged individuals drift into non-engagement. By combining passion and purpose, talents and skills, into an aligned career, we most likely to experience full engagement.

Choose Happiness

Many consider themselves to be powerless when it comes to choices. But the fact is we all have control over our choices. We might take a job that we don't particularly like, in order to pay the bills in the short term, but to settle there for the rest of our days is a choice. We can choose to live the life we feel we were destined for, or settle for something less: the choice is ours. Where we are today is where we have chosen to be. If we prefer to be in a different place, then it's up to us to make it happen.

Career engagement is about life engagement. Get excited about living a full life, and you will make sure that your working years will also be lived fully. Personally speaking, I want to be:

- Known by my children as the one who threw their mother, fully dressed, into the pool

- Known as the man who, in board shorts and thongs, grabbed his unsuspecting girl on a summer's afternoon and danced the rumba with her in the bar of a five star hotel

- Known for laughing, and for being the childlike 50 year-old whose mother still asks, "Will you ever grow up?"

- Known for driving around a roundabout multiple times, with my kids yelling, and their mother threatening to throw up

- The one to outlast all the twenty year-olds on the dance floor

How do you want to live your life? What do you want to be known for?

Adapting to Culture and Leadership

A number of years ago, a woman at a country hotel asked whether I was gay. I promptly told her that no, I was not gay, and that I had a wife and four children. When I mentioned this to a client, she said, "Ray, it's because of the clothes you wear". I said, "But I am wearing clothes that people wear in the country" (I was very much acculturated by city living). "But your boots are always clean", she said. I only had to be told once. Since then no one has questioned me about my sexual preferences having now adapted to country culture.

At work, much the same thing happens. People are quick to fit in, and adapt accordingly. Left to its own devices, however, the workplace culture can quickly head towards mediocrity, or worse. The leader of the high performing industrial firm I initially mentioned made no provision for sloppy engagement practices. Employees were engaged, on the path to full engagement, or on the path to the door. As leader, he set the tone for excellence. The manufacturer, on the other hand, allowed people to act in a non-engaged or disengaged fashion, and paid the price for it – eventually closing up shop. Leadership sets the engagement tone and, given that the Gallup study identified only 17% of leaders as being actually engaged, it seems an awfully long way to the top.

Here are some thoughts about how to create a culture where engagement can thrive.

- Make the environment a fun and enjoyable place to be

- Recognise and reward staff achievement

- Set the performance bar high, and work with your people to achieve the standard

- Create an advancement path, provide training opportunities, stretch targets, give small project responsibility, and help staff to be all that they can be

- Listen to your employees' suggestions for improvement and take action, as appropriate

- Take an active interest in your people, seek to understand their internal drivers and motivators, and work with them accordingly

- Express how much you value people's contributions

- Conduct performance reviews on a regular basis–preferably quarterly. They need to be two-way discussions, perhaps held during a lunch for key people

- If you incentivise, try to tailor rewards to the individual internal motivators, or to team performances

- Work towards consistency in team meetings, sharing your vision, company values, and goals

- Lead with transparency, openness, and honesty

- Eat together. I have observed in my consulting work, that those who engage in social activities, particularly around food, tend to demonstrate higher engagement than those who don't. This factor is also recognised in the Australian Workplace Awards.

- Provide benefits other than merely financial considerations. These might include the opportunity to work from home a couple of days a week, a move towards performance-based, rather than purely time-based work practices, or flexible hours.

Attitude: It's your choice

In his book Man's Search For Meaning, Victor Frankl writes"Everything can be taken from a man but one thing: the last of the human freedoms— to choose one's attitude in any given set of circumstances, to choose one's own way."[1]

We choose the attitude we bring to our work. We might want to change the work we do in the future, but in the present, we choose what we bring to it.

---

[1] Viktor E. Frankl, Man's Search for Meaning (Boston: Beacon Press, 1959)

So what can you choose to do?

- **Seek to outperform yourself** – even in the most mundane tasks of the day

- **See yourself as self-employed**, as the CEO of your own corporation. Treat your work like your own business, and treat yourself as a valuable commodity. When you see yourself this way, you bring power back to you; when you make empowering choices, you become more valuable to your employer.

- **Give your absolute best.** A CEO was once asked how many people worked in his company. He responded "About half of them". Don't be in the other half. Find out what management's expectations are, meet them, and then exceed them. When you become valuable you are more likely to rise to the top, and have increased responsibility and input. You are more likely to receive wage increases and be one of the last to be laid off in the event of a downturn.

- **Establish weekly goals** for yourself, both at work and at home.

In closing, I'd like to tell you about a man called Adrian. He was a big fellow, 6'5" tall, who dreamed of owning a cattle station one day. He pursued his dream relentlessly. An interview in an investment magazine reported him as saying, "I know that anything I believe in is achievable, and the situation we're in today is due to our accumulated decisions, and not to external circumstances". Adrian was a man who took engagement seriously – in both his personal and business worlds. Tragically, at age thirty-eight, his life ended in a car accident. This is an excerpt from his eulogy:

"He was just big. Everything about him was big. The houses he lived in, the cars he drove, and the amount of rum he could drink. It was all big. He had a roundabout in front of his house the size of a city roundabout. His business was big. His plans were big.

His dreams and goals – BIG.

His love for his family – BIG

His love for people – BIG

His love of life and living it to the max – BIG

The way he died – BIG

The hole he's leaving in our lives – BIG

Our gratitude to God for giving us the gift of knowing this man call Adrian …– BIG"

This big man was my little brother. A man who impressed me in everything he applied his focus and efforts to. He lived a big and full life, and was someone for whom anything less than full engagement just wasn't an option.

16

Twenty Insights That Will Significantly Change Your Organisation

All leaders have a desire to work with people who are enthusiastic, pliable, skilled (or willing to develop skills), motivated, and who demonstrate high energy and care in their work. They want people who will treat the job as if it were their own business or organisation, take personal responsibility for their failures, think for themselves, and give 100% while on the job.

In more than 30 years of coaching others, I have gained many insights. Here are some of the key things, which, if adopted, can significantly and often dramatically bring about a change of course for the individual, the team, or the whole organisation.

1. Tough Love Leadership is a leadership style that I have seen work extremely effectively. Team members know they are valued (the 'love'), but also understand that mediocrity is not tolerated (the 'tough').

2.   If you see your job as babysitting, then babysitting it will be. If you see your role as nurturing individuals to achieve greatness, then you will gain so much more.

3.   Help the 'wrong' people to exit the bus. There are plenty of other buses that will take them

4.   Raise the bar. Expect the best from your people.

5.   Team members value having their say. Create an environment where employees can contribute to the ongoing direction and decisions of the company.

6.   Organisations that eat together and create social events tend to enjoy a better workplace culture

7.   Employees want owners and managers that are accessible and personable

8.   Even failure should be celebrated for those who attempt something new; at least they were thinking and acting.

9.   Spend more time on the recruitment process. If you take short cuts up front, you will pay for them further down the track

10.   Hire an employee, based on the whole person, not just technical skills

11. If employees are chosen for their enthusiasm and teach-ability, their skill growth and subsequent mastery will be quicker and easier

12. Employees want to be treated as people not merely as workers

13. Employees don't just have a work life. As much as we would like to believe they can leave their personal baggage at the door, many simply bring it in with them

14. Match employees' behaviour and enjoyment factors to their role

15. Don't promote people beyond their strengths and abilities. Just because they are good technicians doesn't necessarily mean they will be good managers.

16. Some employees are grateful for a demotion or a sideways shift. Some would prefer less money if they can work in their 'sweet spot'.

17. Employees generally like to know how they are performing, and how they can improve

18. You can't make a slow horse speed up; the same is true for employees

19. About motivation:

- Some are motivated by money, others by time with their family; some want the freedom to travel, others want to expand their careers, or increase their intellectual capacity.

- Understand what motivates people, then work with them, and incentivise them accordingly.

- External motivation – whether it comes from rah-rah public speakers, financial rewards, or other extrinsic force – has limited longevity.

- Enduring motivation happens when someone is fuelled by inner desire and passion, enjoy their tasks and have a sense of 'this is what I was made for'.

20. Your workplace is a direct reflection of its leaders. The better you are with people, the better your workplace will be.